Tiny Tea Parties!

CUTE & EASY ERS

Mini Food and Tiny Tea Parties That Look Good Enough To Eat!

Contributors

Amanda Mumbray

Following a career in finance, Amanda Mumbray launched her cake business in 2010 and has gone from strength to strength, delighting customers with her unique bespoke creations and winning several Gold medals at various International Cake Shows. Amanda's **Clever Little Cupcake** company is based near Manchester, UK:
www.cleverlittlecupcake.co.uk

Elina Prawito

Elina Prawito is a cake designer based in Auckland, New Zealand. Her passion for cake design started when she made her son's 1st birthday cake in 2007 and fell in love with sugar art and cake design. 3 years later **bake-a-boo cakes** was born! You can view more of Elina's stunning work at:
www.bakeaboo.com

Lesley Grainger

Lesley Grainger has been imaginative since birth and has baked since she was old enough to hold a spatula. When life-saving surgery prompted a radical rethink, Lesley left a successful corporate career to pursue her passion for cake making. Lesley is based in Greenock, Scotland. Say 'hello' at:
www.lesleybakescakes.co.uk

First published in 2014 by Kyle Craig Publishing

Text and illustration copyright © 2014 Kyle Craig Publishing

Editor: Alison McNicol

Design: Julie Anson

ISBN: 978-1-908-707-43-7

A CIP record for this book is available from the British Library.

A Kyle Craig Publication

www.kyle-craig.com

Contents

Welcome!

Welcome to **'Tiny Tea Parties'**, the latest title in the **Cute & Easy Cake Toppers Collection**.

Each book in the series focuses on a specific theme, and here we have compiled a gorgeous selection of beautiful cake toppers that can be used for all kinds of celebrations!

Whether you're an absolute beginner or an accomplished cake decorator, these projects are suitable for all skill levels, and we're sure that you will have as much fun making them as we did!

Enjoy!

Fondant/Sugarpaste/Gumpaste

Fondant/Sugarpaste – Ready-made fondant, also called ready to roll icing, is widely available in a selection of fantastic colours. Most regular cake decorators find it cheaper to buy a larger quantity in white and mix their own colours using colouring pastes or gels. Fondant is used to cover entire cakes, and as a base to make modelling paste for modelling and figures (see below).

Modelling Paste – Used throughout this book. Firm but pliable and dries faster and harder than fondant/sugarpaste. When making models, fondant can be too soft so we add CMC/Tylose powder to thicken it.

Gumpaste – Also known as 'Florist Paste'. More pliable than fondant, but dries very quickly and becomes quite hard, so it is widely used for items like flowers that are delicate but need to hold their shape when dry. Gumpaste can be made by adding Gum-Tex/Gum Tragacanth to regular fondant.

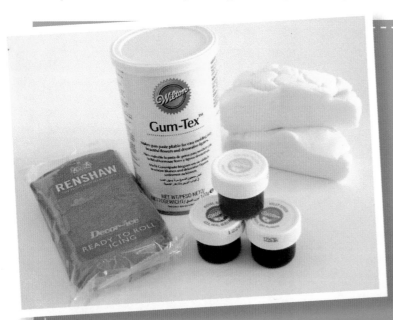

How to Make Modelling Paste

Throughout this book we refer to 'paste', meaning modelling paste. You can convert regular shop-bought fondant into modelling paste by adding CMC/Tylose powder, which is a thickening agent.

Add approx 1 tsp of CMC/Tylose powder to 225g (8oz) of fondant/sugarpaste. Knead well and leave in an airtight freezer bag for a couple of hours.

Add too much and it will crack. If this happens, add in a little shortening (white vegetable fat) to make it pliable again.

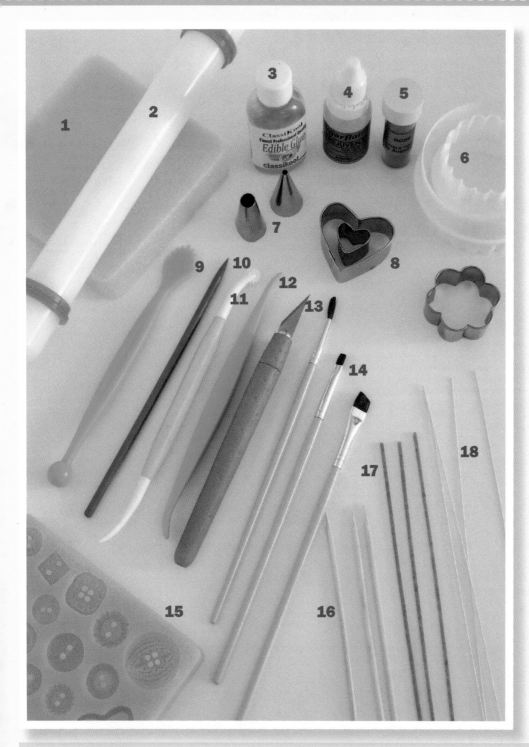

1 Foam Pad – holds pieces in place while drying.

2 Rolling pin – acrylic works better than wooden when working with fondant/paste.

3 Edible glue – essential when creating models. See below.

4 Rejuvenator spirit – mix with food colourings to create an edible paint.

5 Petal Dust, pink – for adding a 'blush' effect to cheeks.

6 Round and scalloped cutters – a modelling essential.

7 Piping nozzles – used to shape mouths and indents.

8 Shaped cutters – various uses.

9 Ball tool/serrated tool – another modelling essential.

10 Small pointed tool – used to create details like nostrils and holes.

11 Quilting tool – creates a stitched effect.

12 Veining tool – for adding details to flowers and models.

13 Craft knife/scalpel – everyday essential.

14 Brushes – to add finer details to faces.

15 Moulds – create detailed paste buttons, fairy wings and lots more.

16 Wooden skewers – to support larger models.

17 Spaghetti strands – also used for support.

18 Coated craft wire – often used in flower making.

Edible Glue

Whenever we refer to 'glue' in this book, we of course mean 'edible glue'. You can buy bottles of edible glue, which is strong and great for holding larger models together. You can also use a light brushing of water, some royal icing, or make your own edible glue by dissolving ¼ teaspoon tylose powder in 2 tablespoons warm water. Leave until dissolved and stir until smooth. This will keep for up to a week in the refrigerator.

Making Faces

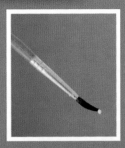

A veining tool will create indents for features.

The end of a piping nozzle can create a great smile shape.

When adding tiny pieces of fondant for eyes, use a moist fine brush.

Edible pens can be used to draw on simple features.

Pink petal dust adds blush to cheeks.

The faces featured in this book vary in terms of detail and difficulty. If you're a complete beginner, you may opt to use edible pens to draw on simple features. As your confidence grows, you can use fondant for eyes and pupils, edible paint for lashes, or combine the two for some great detailing.

Adding Hair

A really cute way to personalise any cake is to make the hair on your model to match the birthday girl – and create a mini-me to top the cake! Are they blonde or brunette? Wear pigtails or curls? So many possibilities!

Side Ponytail

Cute Pigtails

Long Hair

Materials

Modelling paste:
White, Pink, Baby blue,
Egg yellow, Flesh,
Caramel, Red, Dark
Brown, Black, Green
Food colouring: white
Petal dust: pink, brown,
silver
Piping gel
Rejuvenator spirit
Edible glue

Tools

Craft knife/scalpel
Bamboo skewer
Toothpicks
Florist wire, 18 gauge
Fluted pastry circle
Cone tools
Veining tool
Ball tool
Small flower former
Small circle cutters
Plunger blossom cutter
Square cutters
Fine paintbrush

1 First, let's make our birthday girl. You can also make a boy following the steps on page 33.

2 Roll two sausages of paste for the legs. Insert a bamboo skewer to take the body. Add a strip of white for the socks, and two sausages of paste for the shoes.

3 Using a fluted pastry circle, cut out two discs, and frill the edges with the ball tool. Add a little edible glue to top of the legs, and place the frilled skirt over the skewer.

4 Make a fat sausage and hollow out the neckline with your fingers.

5 Cut a thin strip of paste and attach around the waist. Flatten a small ball of paste, and make two button holes with the end of a toothpick.

6 Fill in the neck area with a little paste and pinch up the skewer to create a neck.

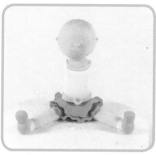

7 Roll a ball of paste for the head, and add three tiny balls for the ears and nose. Gently indent the ears with the cone tool. Roll a thin sausage and secure around the neckline.

8 Roll two sausages, indenting slightly in the middle and towards the end to create a wrist. Make four cuts to make the fingers.

9 Position the arms on the body and glue in place.

10 For the lips, roll out a tiny ball of pink paste. Make a hole with the end of a toothpick and make lip markings with the veining tool. Paint in the eyes, and add blush to the cheeks.

11 Cut out a circle of paste for the hair, and mark with the end of the veining tool. Cut out a small blossom, and paint in details on the bodice and skirt.

12 Roll out two tapered sausages and mark on the hair detail. Glue pigtails in place.

13 Roll out two tiny balls for each pigtail bobble. Glue in place.

14 Roll out a cone shape, and a small ball for the pom pom. Paint in the detail and attach to the top of the head.

15 And now for the birthday cake!

16 Cut out two thick circles of paste in a neutral cake colour.

17 Cut a further two thinner circles from white and red, and sandwich them all together.

18 Roll out some paste, and just slightly mark the paste with the same pastry cutter, being careful not to cut the paste.

19 Using the circle mark as a guide, cut out the runny icing effect making sure not to go inside the circle.

20 Place the icing on the cake, and make 4 holes ready to insert the candles. Roll out a thin sausage and cut four candles, leaving them for a while to firm up.

21 Insert the candles into the cake, adding four tiny teardrops of paste for the flames.

22 Paint on some sprinkles.

23 Now for the ice cream sundae!

24 Roll out a cone shape, insert a toothpick and clip the end of it, leaving just a little bit of it exposed.

25 Cut out a small circle and, with the ball tool, roll it around the centre of the circle so it cups.

26 Insert over the toothpick.

27 Roll three balls of paste for the ice cream.

28 Roll out a sausage of paste, flattening slightly.

29 Insert the sausage shape into the side of the sundae dish, to look like the end of a spoon, and paint silver.

30 Now for the cute mini cupcakes!

31 Roll out three tapered cone shapes and flatten to resemble cupcake bases.

32 Roll out a long sausage of paste and spiral the sausage around the top of the cupcake base.

33 Add a small ball for the cherry.

34 Paint on some sprinkles.

35 Cut a small circle and roll a tapered cone, marking some detail at the base of the cone.

36 Assemble the cake stand upside down. Insert a toothpick to keep it together, and to give stability once on the cake. Leave to dry completely before adding the cupcakes.

37 Teeny tiny cookies!

38 Cut out a circle of paste, and mark in the centre with a smaller circle cutter. Place in the flower former.

39 Paint some detail on the plate, and set aside to dry for a few hours.

40 Cut out the cookies using a small circle cutter.

41 Paint on the chocolate chips.

42 Assemble the cookies on the plate.

The Cake

43 Anyone for a coke float?

44 Roll out two tapered cone shapes.

45 Cut the florist wire into two small lengths and, using a tiny ball of paste, roll the ball around the wire, leaving the end exposed.

46 Insert the wires in to the top of the cups.

47 Paint some detail on to the cups and straws.

48 Pain some bubbles using a toothpick dipped in food colouring.

49 Ham sandwiches are always popular at a party!

50 Cut out a circle of paste, and mark in the centre with a smaller circle cutter. Place in the flower former.

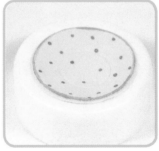

51 Paint some detail on the plate, and set aside to dry for a few hours.

52 Cut out three squares of paste.

53 Cut them all diagonally.

54 Cut out the same size squares in pink paste, cutting diagonally.

55 Cut out the same size squares in pale green, cut diagonally, and frill the edges with the ball tool.

56 Assemble the sandwiches and glue together.

57 Arrange them on the plate, and dust the crusts with the brown petal dust.

58 Every birthday party needs hats and streamers!

59 Roll out two cones for the hats.

60 Add two small balls for the pom-poms, gluing in place

61 Paint on some cute details.

62 Cut long thin strips in various colours.

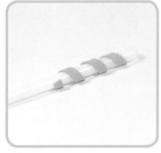
63 Wrap the strips around a cel stick or a paint brush handle. Leave to dry.

64 Once dried, slide off the stick.

65 Jelly time!

66 Cut out a circle of paste, and mark in the centre with a smaller circle cutter. Place in the flower former.

67 Paint some detail on the plate, and set aside to dry for a few hours.

68 Roll out a ball of paste and flatten slightly.

69 Mark some detail up the sides.

70 Roll out a smaller ball of paste, marking detail up the sides, and indenting the top with a circle cutter.

71 Place the smaller ball on top of the large ball and glue in place.

72 Place the jelly on the plate, and paint with a little piping gel to make it look glossy.

The Cupcakes

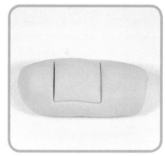

1 Every birthday girl and boy hopes for presents!

2 Roll out a thick sausage of paste, and indent with a square cutter.

3 With a sharp knife, follow the marks and cut out a cube shape.

4 Cut out two thin strips and arrange as if the parcel is wrapped with ribbon.

5 Cut out a rectangle shape, and make slits all the way along the middle, being careful not to cut through to the edges.

6 Moisten one side and fold in half lengthways. Make sure the cuts don't stick together.

7 Roll up the strip to make a loopy bow and glue in place.

8 Attach the bow to the top of the present, and secure to a disc of sugarpaste.

9 Birthday balloons!

10 Roll out a tapered ball.

11 Add a very small ball at the base of the balloon, and insert a paintbrush to make a small hole.

12 Roll out a long thin sausage of paste for the string, and insert into the hole.

13 Fashion a small bow from the same sausage of paste and secure to the base of the balloon.

14 Attach to a paste disc, and paint some white marks to make it look shiny.

15 Mmmmm, donuts!

16 Roll out a sausage of paste and cut both ends straight.

17 Secure both ends together with a little water or edible glue.

18 Cut out a circle of paste, and remove the centre with a smaller circle cutter.

19 Pull the edge of the circles with your fingers to create a drippy icing effect and attach to the top of the donut. Make another one on a contrasting colour.

20 Paint on some sprinkles.

21 Secure to a disc of modelling paste.

22 Lovely birthday lollipops!

23 Roll out two long sausages in different colours.

24 Twist the two sausages together.

25 Spiral the paste to form a circle.

26 Cut a sausage to make the stick, and glue to the circle.

27 Make a similar lollipop in a different colour.

28 Attach both to a disc of sugarpaste.

29 Anyone for a French macaron?

30 Roll out two small balls of paste.

31 Cut the balls in half and sandwich together with a circle of white paste in between. Fluff the filling with the end of a paintbrush.

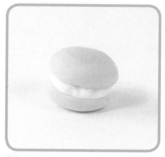

32 Make another macaron in the same way using a contrasting colour.

33 Attach them all to a disc of modelling paste.

34 And finally, a tiny birthday cake!

35 Roll out a ball of paste, and flatten to make a cake shape.

36 Using a craft knife, cut out a wedge of "cake".

37 Cut a thin strip of paste and fill in the centre of the wedge and also the slice of cake, gluing in place.

38 Roll two very thin sausages to make the filling and glue in place.

39 Roll tiny little balls to create the frosting on the top.

40 Make a candle, as before, and insert into the top of the cake by making a hole with the end of a paintbrush.

Now set up your cupcakes with the main cake for a delicious Teeny Tiny Birthday Party!

Materials

Fondant covered cake
Modelling paste:
White, Baby pink, Sky
blue, Green, Scarlet,
Yellow, Red, Kiwi, Brown,
Honey Gold
Edible paint: gold, silver
Petal dust: brown
Piping gel
Rejuvenator spirit
Edible glue

Tools

Craft knife/scalpel
Toothpick
White lollipop stick
Small cocktail straw
Florist wire (approx. 24
gauge)
Veining tool
Ball tool
Quilting tool
Small cutters: round,
square
Small fluted cookie cutters
Small paintbrush

1 Start with your small fondant covered cake. Your cake should have a flat top in order to properly set the decorations on top

2 The tablecloth should be cut larger than your cake diameter to provide a decent overlap/drape. A cake board makes a perfect cutting template.

3 Roll the paste out and, using your circular template, cut your tablecloth piece.

4 Use the quilting tool around the edge of your tablecloth to add detail.

5 Lay the tablecloth over your cake, gently placing into evenly spaced folds.

6 To create the teapot, roll a ball of white paste. Allow to dry a little.

7 Use your knife to cut this ball into a base and lid.

8 To create the spout, roll a small sausage of white paste. Using your fingers, tease this into the shape shown. Allow to dry.

9 To create the handle, roll a small sausage of white paste. Using your fingers, tease this into the shape shown. Allow to dry lightly.

10 Attach all pieces together and add a small ball of paste to the lid. Allow to dry.

11 To create the milk jug, roll a ball of white sugarpaste.

12 Using your fingers, work into the shape shown – a little like a flat-topped hourglass.

13 Tease a spout from this shape by pulling gently with your fingers. Press a small indentation into the centre too.

14 To create the handle, roll a small sausage of white paste. Using your fingers, tease this into the shape shown. Allow to dry lightly.

 **15** Attach to the milk jug and allow to dry.

 **16** To create the sugar bowl, roll a ball of white sugarpaste. Allow to dry a little.

 **17** Use your knife to cut this ball into a base and lid.

 **18** Add a small ball of paste to the lid to create a handle. Allow to dry.

 **19** To create a teacup, cut a small circle of paste.

 **20** Place this circle over your ball tool.

 **21** Tease the paste over the ball tool to form a cup shape. Press on a flat surface to flatten the bottom of your cup.

 **22** Once dry, use your scalpel tool to trim the edges, if required.

 **23** To create the handle, roll a small sausage of white sugarpaste. Using your fingers, tease this into the shape shown. Allow to dry lightly.

 **24** Glue to the teacup and allow to dry.

 **25** For the plates, cut two circles of differing sizes from modelling paste.

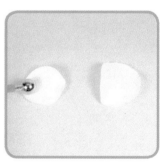 **26** Use your ball tool to lightly thin at the edges then cut again with your circle cutters to bring back to their original size.

 **27** With your ball tool again, roll an indentation into the centre of each piece. They will start to look a little like bowls.

 **28** Turn your plates over and gently press down on the rounded centre...

 **29** Flip back over and now your pieces should be a little flatter and look more like plates. Dry on a flat surface.

 **30** To create the vase, roll a fat sausage shape of paste.

 **31** Use your fingers to mould this into an hourglass shape, as shown. Form a rounded indentation on top – no need to make this too deep.

 **32** To create the flowers, cut small blossom shapes from pink paste and thin each one with your ball tool.

 **33** Take small pieces of florist wire and attach a small ball of paste to the end of each one.

 **34** Thread the wire through the centre of your thinned out flower shape.

 **35** Fold your flower over and around the ball shape.

 **36** Create a bunch of your little flowers, enough to display in your vase.

 **37** To create leaves, roll small tapered sausages of paste as shown.

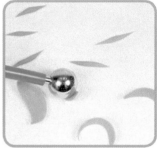 **38** Use your ball tool to gently thin and curl these pieces.

 **39** Carefully add all items to your vase. Insert the flowers individually then add leaves to fill in the spaces.

 **40** To create the cake stand, cut two fluted circles of sugarpaste.

 **41** Gently thin the scalloped edges with your ball tool, as shown.

 **42** Use a cocktail straw (or similar) to punch holes in your cake stand plates. Create a hole on the centre of each piece through which to insert your lolly stick.

 **43** Insert your lolly stick into a piece of paste to create a stable base for your cake stand. Trim to size desired.

 **44** Thread and glue the cake plates onto the stand. You may wish to add a small piece of paste underneath the top plate to prevent slipping.

 **45** To create a tiny teaspoon, roll a thin piece of paste. Fold one end a little back on itself and press into a little spoon shape.

 **46** Use a very small ball tool to create an indentation.

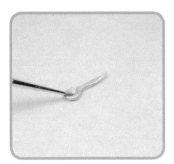   

47 Paint with edible silver paint.

48 Use your edible gold paint to highlight details on your items. On the teapot lid, paint the handle and rim. (See Steps 75 onwards for painted flower details.)

49 On the milk jug, paint a thin gold line around the rim.

50 On the sugarbowl lid, paint the handle and rim.

51 Paint the rim of your teacup.

52 Colour piping gel to resemble tea and carefully add to teacup.

53 Paint the rim of your plates.

54 Add polka dot details to your vase...

55 ...and a gold ball to the top of your cake stand!

56 To create a napkin, cut a small square of white paste.

57 Gently thin the edges with your ball tool...

58 ...and add stitching detail with your quilting tool.

59 Fold over and allow to dry.

60 To create the sandwiches, cut two light brown squares of sugarpaste and one smaller green square.

61 Lightly texturise your 'bread' by pricking the brown pieces with a toothpick.

62 Press and roll the tip of your toothpick around the outer of the green square to create a frilled lettuce-like appearance.

 **63** Add all pieces together and cut into sandwich quarters.

 **64** You can add a brush of brown petal dust for extra detail.

 **65** To create the scones, cut two small circles of beige paste.

 **66** Create indentations around the edges of each piece.

 **67** Cut circles of cream coloured paste in the same size as your scone...

 **68** ...and red circles too. This will form the jam – you can tease this slightly with your fingers to suggest oozing!

 **69** Attach all pieces together and dust the top of your scone with brown petal dust.

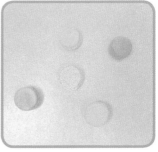 **70** To create the macarons, cut small circles of pastel coloured paste.

 **71** Use your fingers to 'round' the edges of each piece...

 **72** ...and use your toothpick to lightly prick the sides.

 **73** Create the filling by cutting flatter, white circles of paste.

 **74** Attach all pieces together – voila...pretty macarons!

 **75** For painted flower details on tea set, use a scrap piece of dried paste to practice on first! Paint an abstract blossom shape in pale pink...

 **76** ...then paint a few darker pink 'swirls' on top.

 **77** With a clean, damp paintbrush, gently blend these lines together.

 **78** For the leaves, paint a green outline only then with a clean, damp paintbrush lightly drag this outline inwards and blend.

Vintage Tea Party Cupcakes

Materials

Modelling paste:
White, Cream, Baby pink,
Bright Pink, Sky blue,
Green, Yellow, Orange,
Red, Green, Beige, Lilac
Petal dust: brown
Edible paint: gold & silver
Edible pen: black, green
Piping gel
White non-pareils
Icing/powdered sugar
Confectioners glaze
Edible glue

Tools

Craft knife/scalpel

Veining tool

Ball tool

Small, round cutters

Small blossom cutter

Small paintbrush

1 For the Victoria Sponge cake, roll a thick piece of deep beige paste and cut two circles. Shape the top of one piece with a cupped palm to resemble a domed cake shape.

2 Roll a thin piece of cream paste and cut with the same cutter as before. This will create your cake 'filling'.

3 Attach this 'filling to the cake base piece, softly shaping over the sides with your fingers.

4 Brush the top cake piece with brown petal dust.

5 Add red piping gel to the bottom of your 'cake' to resemble the 'jam'!

6 Sandwich the halves together and sprinkle powdered/icing sugar over the top.

7 To create a little strawberry decoration, roll a small teardrop of red paste. Cut a tiny green blossom shape and roll a tiny 'stem' too.

8 To create the cake slice, cut an arrow shape from white paste. Brush with edible silver paint.

9 For the Swiss Roll, cut a rectangle of beige paste...

10 ...and cut a larger rectangle of brown paste.

11 Attach the pieces together...

12 ...bringing the lighter layer close to the edge of where the 'roll' will begin. Tuck the start of the roll over tightly...

13 ...and roll.

14 Trim the ends of your creation then cut a 'slice' for decorative purposes.

15 For the fruit flan, cut a circle of light brown paste.

16 Insert this carefully into a slightly larger round cutter and use the rounded end of a veining tool to 'pinch' the edges in, creating a 'crust base' for your flan. Allow to dry.

17 Remove the 'flan base' and add indents to create an authentic pastry look. Use a round cutter to press the tool against as this will minimize the risk of tearing the paste.

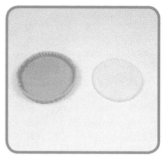

18 Cut a piece of cream paste to fit inside the flan base and glue in place.

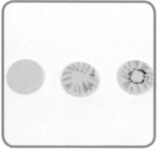

19 Cut approx. 12-15 small circles of green paste and allow to dry a little. Mark these with green edible ink pen then add a small circle of black dots to resemble kiwi slices.

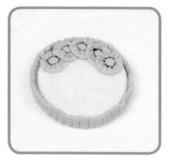

20 Arrange these around the outer edge and glue in place.

21 Cut a selection of apricot coloured circles (same size as before) and cut these in half.

22 Arrange and glue these in the centre of your 'flan'.

23 Roll tiny balls of red paste and attach to the centre. Brush the 'fruit' with some confectioners glaze to create a realistic shine.

24 For the eclairs, roll equal sized balls of dark beige paste.

25 Shape these into sausages.

26 Take a piece of white paste and quickly pull it apart. This will leave the ragged edge you need.

27 Trim this ragged edge off.

28 Cut a split into each of your sausage shapes. From your ragged white paste, trim a small piece and attach to the inside of your 'éclair'.

29 Roll a pliable brown sausage of paste and lay on top of your bun.

30 Use your fingers to tease this topping out across the bun.

31 You can create an alternative look using pale pink paste and a thin roll of white paste, arranged to emulate icing.

32 Another alternative can be made by adding a stripe of red piping gel. Complete the look by lightly sprinkling powdered/icing sugar across the top of your bun.

33 To create empire biscuits, cut small round pieces of beige paste.

34 To half of these, add a little dab of red piping gel.

   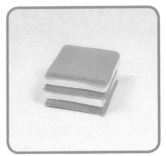

35 To the remaining pieces, cut slightly smaller white circles and attach these on top.

36 Complete by adding a cherry on top (a small ball of red paste) and sandwich both pieces together.

37 To create some petit fours, cut equal sized squares of contrasting paste. Allow to dry a little.

38 Layer together, attaching as you go. Five layers are ideal.

  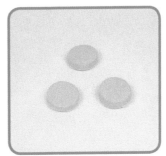 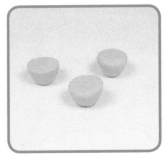

39 Depending on the size of decoration you require, you may be able to cut this arrangement into four, providing four separate petit fours.

40 Decorate your little cakes using tiny paste blossoms or a sprinkling of non-pareils.

41 To create cupcakes, cut small round pieces of beige paste.

42 Use your fingers to shape these into cupcake base forms.

43 Use a knife or sharp tool to create cupcake case-like indentations around the outsides.

44 Roll long, thin pieces of colourful paste.

45 Glue one end to the centre of your cupcake base and begin to coil around, creating a swirl effect.

46 Finish by adding a tiny ball of contrasting paste and brushing with confectioners glaze to add shine.

1 Begin by creating paste discs to display your Ice Cream Shop items.

2 Use a 68mm round cutter to make your base disc in white.

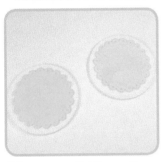

3 Next cut a slightly smaller fluted round cutter to create the colourful overlay. Glue together and leave to dry.

4 To create the ice cream cone, start by taking a piece of beige paste.

5 Roll this into a small cone shape which will fit comfortably on your discs.

6 Mark lines in a criss-cross pattern to create a 'waffle' effect.

7 To create the ice cream, take small pieces of dark pink/red, pale pink and white paste...

8 ...and combine them together. Don't completely blend the colours together as you want to achieve a 'streaked' look.

9 Roll this into a long sausage shape...

10 ...then, on a flat surface, twist upwards to create a 'whippy' shape. Glue as you go.

11 Complete the look by creating a flaked chocolate. Take a tiny piece of brown paste, roll then score with your veining tool. Cut to size.

12 Assemble all pieces together and glue to the disc.

13 For the 'banana split', first make the sundae dish. Create a form over which to shape your dish from a firm, dry sausage of paste.

14 Take a thin piece of paste and lay it over your form, trimming into shape as you go.

15 Use a sausage shape of yellow paste to make the banana. Add some banana-like markings, curve slightly and taper at the ends. Ensure that it fits your sundae dish.

16 For the ice cream scoops, take three small balls of contrasting paste.

17 Bunch some toothpicks together and wrap with a small elastic band.

18 Using a jabbing motion, texturise your ice cream scoops. They may flatten a little, so lightly roll back into shape.

19 Attach the banana and scoops to the dried sundae dish.

20 Place a small amount of royal icing into your piping bag, with a small star shaped tip attached.

21 Pipe three small 'swirls' on top of your 'ice cream'.

22 While the icing is still wet, sprinkle some multi-coloured non-pareils on top.

23 Finish with a 'cherry' created by rolling a tiny ball of red paste with a sliver of brown paste attached to the top.

24 To create the 'knickerbocker glory' ice cream sundae, roll a piece of paste into the shape shown to form your 'sundae glass'.

25 Use your veining tool to make ridges on the sides.

26 Flatten a round pad of paste to form the base of your sundae glass. Glue and allow to dry.

27 Create a fan-shaped wafer by cutting the shape shown from paste. Mark with your veining tool and dry.

28 Make a 'cherry' by rolling a small red ball and adding a sliver of brown paste.

29 Using your royal icing as before, create a large swirl on top of your sundae.

30 Finish by sprinkling with multi-coloured non-pareils and attaching the cherry.

31 To create the ice cream bowl, use a round shape as a form over which to dry your bowl shape (we used a small foam ball).

32 Take a thin piece of paste and shape over the form. Use your veining tool to create markings, if desired. Trim the edges.

33 Take a number of small balls of contrasting paste to form your ice cream scoops.

34 Using your toothpick bunch, jab the balls of paste to create a realistic appearance.

35 Once the bowl is dry, form a round pad of paste to create a base.

36 Add the ice cream scoops to the bowl, attaching as you go.

37 Make a 'cherry' by rolling a small red ball and adding a sliver of brown paste.

38 Using your royal icing as before, create a large swirl on top of your 'ice cream bowl'.

39 Finish by sprinkling with multi-coloured non-pareils and attaching the 'cherry'.

40 To create the single coloured ice lolly, cut a rectangle of paste. Ensure that the size is appropriate to your paste disc.

41 To create a single coloured ice lolly, cut a rectangle of paste. Ensure that the size is appropriate to your paste disc.

42 Create a lollipop stick by repeating this process but on a smaller scale. Attach both pieces to your disc.

43 For the two-tone lollies, take contrasting pieces of paste.

44 Roll into thin sausage shapes and twist together.

45 Either cut to form a single 'stick' shaped lolly or roll into a spiral, as shown.

46 Add thin pieces of light brown/beige paste to form lollipop sticks. Glue onto discs.

Petite Picnic

1 Let's start by making your little boy. (You can also see how to make a girl on page 9.)

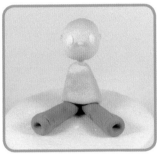

2 Roll two sausages of paste for the legs, marking with a veining tool. Indent holes at the bottom of the legs. Insert a skewer to take the body and head.

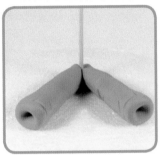

3 Make a cone shape for the body, flattening slightly and insert over the skewer.

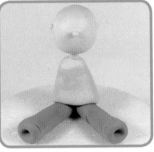

4 Roll a ball for the head, and three tiny balls for the nose and ears. Indent the ears with the smooth end of the cone tool. Glue to head.

5 Make indentations with the thin end of the cone tool for the eyes.

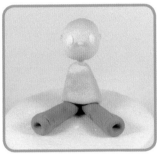

6 Add two elongated white balls for the eyes.

7 Roll out two sausage shapes for the feet, tapering at one end.

8 Glue the feet into the bottom of each leg.

9 Paint in the facial details, and dust the cheeks with a little petal dust.

10 Roll two sausages for the arms, indenting in the middle and at the wrists. Make four cuts and shape the fingers.

11 Make a cone shape, and open up one end with the cone tool.

12 Insert the arms in to the end of the sleeves, and attach to the body.

13 Cut a thin strip and mark with a veining tool. Attach to make the collar of the T-shirt.

14 Cut out a circle of paste for the hair, cutting where desired, and marking on the hair pattern with a veining tool.

The Cake

15 Every picnic starts with a picnic basket!

16 Roll out some paste fairly thickly, and cut into a rectangular shape with a knife.

17 Roll out some brown paste, and then roll over it with the basket weave rolling pin to make the impression. Alternatively, add a weave effect using your veining tool or knife.

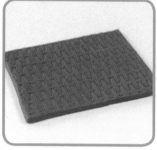

18 Cut four panels for the sides of the basket.

19 Glue the panels to the sides of the rectangle.

20 Roll out two long sausages, twist together, and arrange around the edges of the basket.

21 Cut out a rectangle for the lid, and make the twisted edge as before. Glue and leave it to dry before assembling.

22 Cut out a little strip for the handle, securing at the two far edges, and indent with the end of a paintbrush.

23 Roll out a sausage shape.

24 Use your knife to make diagonal markings along the top of the loaf.

25 Make another, but cut in half, and add a small circle of white to the end.

26 Arrange the bread in the basket, and attach the lid, securing with a little glue.

27 Time for some pies and sausage rolls!

28 Roll out a long sausage shape.

The Cake

29 Cut a thin rectangle shape and place the sausage on top.

30 Wrap the rectangle around the sausage and cut off sections.

31 Make indentations across the top of each sausage roll.

32 Roll out a ball and flatten slightly. Make two marks on top of the pie.

33 Roll two sausages of paste, twist them together, and arrange around the top of the pie to make the crust. Glue in place.

34 Anyone for cherry pie?

35 Cut out a circle of paste and place in the flower former.

36 Roll a ball of red paste, and flatten slightly. Push into the base of the pie.

37 Cut out six longs strips of paste.

38 Attach to the top of the pie in a lattice pattern.

39 Twist two long sausages of paste together.

40 ttach the twisted sausage to the top of the pie to make the crust.

41 Time for tea!

42 Roll out a sausage of paste.

The Cake

43 Cut off both ends to make them flat.

44 Add a small cylinder to the top for the cup part of the flask.

45 Roll out a tiny sausage of paste, and attach to the lid.

46 Make another cylinder of paste, and hollow out the centre with the end of the cone tool. Add a handle as before.

47 Roll out a small ball of brown paste and push into the cup. Paint some detail onto the flask.

48 Grapes and cheese!

49 Roll out a ball shape and flatten slightly.

50 Cut out a wedge using a sharp knife.

51 Make the holes using the small end of the ball tool, or the end of a paintbrush.

52 Roll a teardrop shape of paste.

53 Roll and glue on lots of little balls of paste to create the grapes.

54 Roll a small sausage to make the stalk.

55 Ham salad rolls are always popular at picnics!

56 Cut out a circle of paste, and mark in the centre with a smaller circle cutter. Place in the flower former.

The Cake

57 Paint some detail on the plate, and set aside to dry for a few hours.

58 Roll out four balls of paste. Flatten two completely, and just push the other two slightly, to keep them rounded.

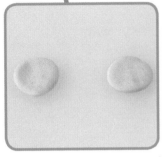

59 Flatten two balls of pink paste to make the slices of ham.

60 Flatten two balls of green paste, and pinch at the edges to make them look thinner, like lettuce.

61 Assemble the rolls.

62 Attach the rolls to the plate.

63 Mmmmm, chicken drumsticks!

64 Cut out a circle of paste, and mark in the centre with a smaller circle cutter. Place in the flower former.

65 Paint some detail on the plate, and set aside to dry for a few hours.

66 Roll out three teardrop shapes.

67 Make tiny holes at the base of each teardrop.

68 Insert small teardrop shapes into the base of each chicken leg, and mark some detail with a cocktail stick.

69 Attach to the plate.

70 Turn over to make more cool picnic food and matching cupcakes!

The Cupcakes

1 Time for a nice cup of tea!

2 Roll out a ball of paste and flatten slightly at the top.

3 To make the lid, roll out a ball of paste and flatten, and attach a tiny ball. Roll out a sausage shape for the handle. Roll a tapered cone for the spout. Glue all in place.

4 Cut out a circle of paste, and mark in the centre with a smaller circle cutter. Place in the flower former.

5 Roll a small ball of paste, and hollow out with the cone tool. Attach a small sausage shape for the handle.

6 Insert a small brown ball into the centre of the cup and push down with the ball tool.

7 Paint on some details and attach to a disc of sugarpaste.

8 And now for a fruit plate!

9 Cut out a circle of paste, and mark in the centre with a smaller circle cutter. Place in the flower former.

10 Paint some detail on the plate, and set aside to dry for a few hours.

11 Roll out a tapered sausage and bend slightly in the middle.

12 Paint on some detail to look like banana markings.

13 Roll out a small ball, and a sausage of brown paste for the apple stalk. Make a hole in the ball and insert the stalk.

14 Attach to the plate, dust one side of the apple with petal dust and glue onto a disc of paste.

15 It's wine o'clock!

16 Roll out a sausage of paste, tapering one end to resemble a bottle.

17 Cut off both ends to make them flat.

18 Add a strip for the neck of the bottle, and a little rectangle for the label.

19 Paint some detail onto the label.

20 Cut a small sausage shape, and make a hole in the centre. Cut a thin strip of paste and wrap around a cocktail stick.

21 Once the spiral has dried, insert into the handle, and paint silver. Attach both items on to a disc of sugarpaste.

22 Every picnic needs a yummy chocolate cake!

23 Cut out three circles for the cake, and two for the filling.

24 Sandwich all the circles together.

25 Cut out a wedge with a sharp knife.

26 Roll lots of little balls for the top edge of the cake and glue in place.

27 Roll out a tiny ball of red, and make a hole on one side. Roll out a very thin sausage of green.

28 Assemble the cherry, and stick on top of the cake.

29 Attach to a disc of sugarpaste, and paint on some sprinkles.

30 What's your favourite flavour of crisps/potato chips?

31 Cut out a square of paste, and flatten one edge with your finger.

32 Cut the flattened edge to make it straight, and also make a slit at the opposite end.

33 Tease the slit open with your fingers and mark little lines down the flattened cut edge.

34 Cut out lots of tiny circles. Pull the circles gently to make them oval, and with a ball tool, gently roll it around the centre of each crisp/potato chip to cup it.

35 Attach a strip across the centre of the bag.

36 Assemble on a disc of sugarpaste, and paint some detail on to the packet.

37 And finally, something for the kids to drink!

38 Roll out a sausage of paste, cutting one end to make it flat.

39 Using the small end of the ball tool, make indentations around the bottom of the bottle.

40 Roll out a tiny ball of paste for the bottle top, and flatten slightly before gluing in place

41 Cut a strip of paste and attach it to the centre of the bottle.

42 Paint on some detail.

Materials

Modelling paste:
White, Red,
Pink, Yellow,
Orange, Brown
Food colouring: black,
blue
Rejuvenator spirit
Edible glue

Tools

Craft knife/scalpel
Veining tool
Cone tool
Small flower former
Small circle cutters
Fine paintbrush

1 Fancy a nice 'full english' breakfast?

2 Cut some very thin strips of red paste. Roll out some white paste. Lay the red strips in a check pattern, and roll over carefully with a rolling pin. Cut two circles for your main discs.

3 Cut out a circle of paste, and mark in the centre with a smaller circle cutter. Place in the flower former.

4 Roll out a very small brown sausage shape, bending slightly in the middle.

5 Roll out a ball of white and a smaller ball of yellow. Flatten both and stick together.

6 Mix some pink paste with a little white but don't mix completely, leaving them looking marbled. Roll and cut two strips of 'bacon'. Mark some lines with a veining tool.

7 For the 'beans', roll lots of tiny orange balls and stick together.

8 Arrange all the items on the plate and paint some detail on to the edge of the plate. Attach to the paste disc.

9 Now for a nice mug of strong tea!

10 Make a cylinder shape, and hollow out slightly with the end of the cone tool.

11 Roll a small ball of paste, and push it into the cup. Roll a small sausage to make the handle.

12 Cut out two rectangular pieces of paste and layer one on top of the other. Make a line down the centre.

13 Fold the paste up like a newspaper.

14 Attach the items to the disc of sugarpaste and paint in the detail on the front of the newspaper.

1 Roll light brown paste to approx. 1.5cm (½") thickness, making sure surfaces are flat and even. Cut it into a rectangle, approx. 7.5cm x 5 cm (3 x 2").

2 Slightly soften the edges using your fingers.

3 Use a quilting tool to mark a line across the middle of the suitcase's front for the opening/zipper, then mark 'stitching' around the edges of the suitcase.

4 For the 'leather' belts and handle, thinly roll out medium brown paste and cut out 2 long strips and one thicker, shorter strip.

5 Glue these to the suitcase. Create small dots with a toothpick. For the locks, roll two small white balls. Attach them either side of the handle.

6 To make the bottom suitcase, you will need a foam board for the suitcase top part and modelling paste for the bottom part.

7 Using the same method as above, cut ivory paste approx. 1.5cm (½") thickness, and 6cm x 4.5cm (2 ⅓ x 1 ¾") to create the base box. Let this dry.

8 Thinly roll mint blue fondant and cut out four rectangle shapes- same length as each side of the base box, but slightly more than its height – see picture. 9.

9 Glue each piece to the base box, starting from the front, then the sides and lastly the back part. Cut away any excess with a sharp knife.

10 To make the top part of the suitcase, cut a foam board the same measurement as the bottom part.

11 Thinly roll ivory paste and attach it to one side of the foam board only. This will be the inside part of the suitcase.

12 Thinly roll mint blue paste and attach it to the back side and edges of the foam board, but leaving the bottom part bare. Cut away any excess.

13 Insert a support toothpick in the back center of the suitcase on a slight angle.

14 Carefully attach the top part of the suitcase onto the bottom part. Leave to dry.

15 To create the suitcase handle and lock, roll out ivory paste into a ball shape and thinly roll medium brown paste and cut into a small strip.

16 Attach them to the suitcase.

17 Position the smaller suitcase onto the top of the bigger suitcase and glue them together.

18 For the mini bunting, thinly roll white paste and cut out 5 square shapes. Let them dry, then write P, A, R, I, S using a black edible pen.

19 Carefully glue them onto the top part of the suitcase.

20 To make the cake plate, cute a circle of white paste. Make small dots using a toothpick around the edges to create some detailing.

21 To make the layer cake, thinly roll white and yellow paste and cut into lots of same sized square shapes.

22 Cut a small daisy shape using a daisy flower plunger cutter and roll a tiny yellow ball.

23 Assemble and glue them layer by layer, alternating colours. Attach the daisy and stick then glaze the yellow candy ball with piping gel.

24 To make the little croissant, roll and cut light brown paste into a long triangle shape. Start rolling from the bottom and finish at the pointy part.

25 Soften the edges and slightly bend the ends of the croissant. Let it dry. Mix the two lustre dusts and dust the top, then glaze with piping gel.

26 To make the bread, roll a small piece of light brown paste into a pointy sausage shape.

27 Make four cuts on the top of the bread. Dust the top part with the brown and yellow mixed dusts then glaze with piping gel.

28 For the cup saucer, thinly roll white paste and cut into a flower shape. Emboss using a smaller size circle cutter and finish off with small dots around the saucer.

29 For the macarons, roll a small ball of pink paste and slightly press down to flatten. Make small dots around the bottom part with a toothpick.

30 To make the filling in white, do the same as above, but make it thinner and flatter. Assemble the macarons.

31 To make the teapot, roll out a round shape of yellow paste.

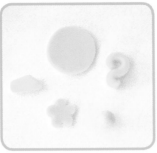

32 Make various shapes as shown in the picture– lid, lid handle, flower, handle.

33 Attach them to the tea pot body. Finish off by creating dots around the teapot's lid using a toothpick.

34 To make the teacup, start by rolling a round cup shape in yellow paste.

35 Using the ball tool, press it down gently to shape the tea cup.

36 Keep pressing the ball tool down and rotate it gently until you get a tea cup look.

37 Cut a mini daisy flower shape and roll out a letter S shape for the handle. Glue both to the tea cup.

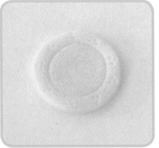

38 To make the saucer, cut a small yellow circle. Slightly emboss it using a smaller size circle cutter and finish it off with small dots around the edge.

39 To add the tea to the teacup, start by rolling a small ball shape of light brown paste.

40 Insert the small ball in the teacup and press it gently with the ball tool.

41 Keep pressing it down and spread it gently until it fills the teacup, then glaze with piping gel to add shine.

42 To make the swiss roll cake, thinly roll dark brown and pink paste and cut each into a long rectangle shape.

43 Place the pink on top of the brown and glue together. Gently roll it up, then slice using a sharp knife then glaze the top with piping gel.

44 Now arrange all the parts on your cake!

Et Voilà! Un petit thé!

RECIPES ♥ TUTORIALS

Cake & Bake ACADEMY
Est. 2014

RESOURCES ♥ INSPIRATION